CONTENTS

THE ART OF THE STUNT

On 24 October 1901, Annie Edson Taylor took a ride in a pickle barrel. It was her 63rd birthday. Taylor climbed inside and was sealed in. Then she was set adrift in a river. The strong current pulled Taylor closer and closer to churning water. Finally, she tumbled over Niagara Falls in New York, USA. The 51-metre (167-foot) drop seemed to promise certain death. Several thousand people showed up to watch the stunt – and to see whether she lived or died.

Daring, record-setting stunts have a long history of grabbing public attention. These stunts range from jumping vehicles over **obstacles** to extreme skydiving to holding one's breath underwater. High-profile stunts are rarely reckless acts, though. Thrill-seekers plan carefully and train hard to prepare. It's the only way to safely test the wonders of human strength, endurance and courage.

obstacle something that gets in the way or prevents someone from doing something

Annie Edson Taylor was rowed to the falls before plunging over in a barrel.

CHAPTER 1

NERVES OF STEEL

On 15 October 2008, American Nik Wallenda went for a bike ride – on a high wire stretched far above the street. He wasn't wearing any safety devices. Near the finish, his back wheel began to slip. He wobbled. A zing of fear instantly swept through the national TV audience.

Wallenda found his balance and took a deep breath. Then he completed the stunt. He had crossed 72 metres (235 feet) at a height of 41 metres (135 feet). He set world records for both distance and height. In 2010 he reset the height record at 73 metres (238 feet).

Nik Wallenda belongs to the seventh **generation** of the Flying Wallendas. They are the most famous family of daredevils the world has ever known. Nik followed in the footsteps of his great-grandfather, Karl Wallenda.

generation group of people born and living at about the same time

In 1928 Karl and his family became the stars of the Ringling Brothers and Barnum & Bailey Circus. When their safety net was lost, the Wallendas went through with their act anyway. Performing without a net, and risking injury or death, became one of their trademarks. "Life is being on the wire, everything else is just waiting," Karl once said. He was 73 when he fell during a 1978 performance and died. But the tragedy hasn't stopped more generations of Wallendas from joining the family business.

FACT

Nik Wallenda holds the record for longest walk on a wire over a waterfall. He set it at Niagara Falls in 2012.

A DAREDEVIL FOR LAUGHS

With his poof of red hair and goofy outfits, Bello Nock has been called "America's Best Clown". But he has also been called "The Ultimate Daredevil". His circus acts feature amazing, heart-stopping stunts.

In 2010 Nock did a high-wire act at sea. He walked on a 1.3-centimetre (0.5-inch) cable placed 79 metres (260 feet) above the deck of a cruise ship. He walked 131 metres (429 feet) along the length of the ship. Guinness World Records said it was the longest tightrope walk not over land.

In an interview Nock said stunt artists must practice four different jobs. First, there is the scientist who dreams up the stunt. Second is the engineer who plans how to do it. Then there is the daredevil willing to take the risk. Lastly, there is the performer who enjoys doing it again and again for an audience.

FACT

The technical term for a "tightrope walker" is a funambulist.

Bello Nock walked on a wire 110 metres (360 feet) high in Biloxi, Mississippi, USA, on 21 June 2012.

THE ENDURANCE ARTIST

American illusionist David Blaine wows people with his illusions. But he is most famous as an **endurance** artist. He has trained his body to control his needs for air, water and food. In one stunt, he was sealed inside a coffin-like box. People could view him through a 2.7-metric ton (3-short ton) water tank that sealed him in. Blaine stayed there for a week, surviving on a few sips of water each day. In 2003 he hung in a clear box by the River Thames in London, UK. He stayed there for 44 days, surviving on just water.

In 2008 Blaine set his first world record by holding his breath. He inhaled pure oxygen beforehand. It built up the oxygen in his blood. Then he climbed into a tank of water. He held his breath there for 17 minutes and 4.4 seconds. Blaine's record has since been broken. But no one has captured the world's imagination for endurance stunts like David Blaine.

FACT

The record for holding one's breath without inhaling pure oxygen is 11 minutes, 35 seconds. Frenchman Stephane Mifsud set the record in 2009.

endurance ability to continue when tired or in pain

David Blaine was suspended above the River Thames in London from 5 September to 19 October in 2003.

CHAPTER 2

ON WHEELS

American daredevil Robert "Evel" Knievel (1938–2007) gained fame as a motorcycle jumper. He jumped his bike over parked cars, trucks, buses and even a pile of rattlesnakes. He wore what looked like a superhero outfit and staged his stunts as big **spectacles**.

Knievel's stunts drew huge audiences to stadiums and TV sets. Viewers held their breath as he raced his Harley-Davidson towards the takeoff ramp. They crossed their fingers as he took off. Sometimes he landed safely. Sometimes he crashed in grand fashion. During his career, Knievel broke 433 bones. That's a world record of its own. Knievel's courage and **showmanship** helped set the stage for even more amazing stunts on wheels.

spectacle big public show

showmanship ability to entertain and perform

Evel Knievel attempted more than 75 ramp-to-ramp motorcycle jumps.

THE LONGEST JUMP ON TWO WHEELS

As a kid, American motorcycle jumper Alex Harvill remembered playing with his dad's Evel Knievel action figure. He grew up racing and jumping BMX bicycles. Then he switched to dirt bikes.

In May 2012 Harvill went from an unknown dirt bike racer to a motorcycle jumping sensation. The 19-year-old sped up a ramp and took off. He cleared 130 metres (425 feet) before his wheels hit ground. The jump smashed the record for ramp-to-dirt distance jumping by 10 metres (33 feet).

FACT

In 2011 Levi LaVallee jumped his snowmobile 125.7 metres (412.5 feet), smashing his own distance record.

Harvill also races
250-cc dirt bikes in
American Motorcycle
Association (AMA)
supercross races.

Harvill plans to continue breaking records. "I owe it to Evel and everyone who has done it before me to keep pushing it as far as I can go," he said.

LONGEST JUMP ON FOUR WHEELS

Motorsport fans got a pre-race thrill on the morning of the 2011 Indy 500. A 30.5-metre (100-foot) tower stood in the speedway's infield. An orange ramp dropped like a giant slide from the top. Waiting there was a racing truck with stunt driver Tanner Foust behind the wheel. He was about to attempt the world record for longest jump by a four-wheeled vehicle.

Months of planning had gone into the stunt. The truck was designed to cut through the air without nose-diving or flipping backwards. Planners tested the angles of the takeoff and landing ramps. Foust practised for three months to get a feel for the truck's power and handling.

Tanner Foust (right) also races rally cars. He caught some air during the 2015 Red Bull Global Rallycross race.

Finally it was the moment of truth. Foust dropped into the ramp to pick up speed. Once the track flattened out, he hit the pedal and sped up past 161 kilometres (100 miles) per hour. Foust raced up the ramp and left the ground behind. He landed 4 seconds later with the world record of 101 metres (332 feet). "For a jump like this, it's all just science," Foust told a reporter.

FACT

In 2004 Danny Way set a world record on a "mega ramp". He jumped 24 metres (79 feet) on his skateboard.

CHAPTER 3

LOOK OUT BELOW!

But what ever happened to Annie Edson Taylor? She was the teacher who went over Niagara Falls in a pickle barrel. Well, the barrel she was in splashed down hard at the base of the falls and banged into some rocks. A boat pulled it to shore and the top was pried open. Taylor, cushioned by a mattress, had a **concussion** and a bloody gash on her head. But she was able to walk away from her stunt.

Later Taylor said, "I would rather face a cannon knowing that I would be blown to pieces than go over the falls again." She had hoped to earn a fortune by giving speeches and writing a book about her stunt, but that never happened. She is famous, though, as the first person to survive going over Niagara Falls.

FACT

Sixteen daredevils have gone over Niagara Falls. Five have died. Today, anyone who attempts the stunt faces prison, fines and possibly death.

Felix Baumgartner became the first skydiver to fall faster than the speed of sound during his 2012 jump.

PAYING THE BILLS

Record-breaking stunts usually cost big money. In 2012 skydiver "Fearless" Felix Baumgartner set a record for the highest free fall with a parachute at about 39 kilometres (24 miles) above the Earth. All his equipment, training and support staff were estimated to have cost millions of dollars.

How could anyone come up with that much money? Baumgartner had a **sponsor**. Some companies pay daredevils to perform stunts that grab the public's attention. In return, these people put the company name and logo on every piece of their clothing and gear. Their stunts are like big advertisements.

concussion injury to the brain caused by a hard blow to the head

sponsor person or company that supports a project

FREE FALL FROM THE STRATOSPHERE

Alan Eustace was already a successful computer scientist. But he was also an aeroplane pilot and skydiver. In 2014 he set out to break Felix Baumgartner's record for the highest-**altitude** free fall parachute jump.

That October, Eustace was attached to a huge helium balloon. He wore a custom-made spacesuit that weighed about 181 kilograms (400 pounds). The balloon lifted off. For more than two hours Eustace dangled below it as it rose into the sky. It carried him into the stratosphere, an upper layer of Earth's **atmosphere**.

Eustace is rolled on a cart while wearing his heavy spacesuit before his record-setting jump.

At an altitude of 41,420 metres (135,892 feet),
Eustace separated himself from the balloon. He
began falling, gaining speed as he fell. During his
free fall, he reached a **velocity** of 1,321 kilometres
(822 miles) per hour – faster than sound travels.
After 4 minutes and 27 seconds, he opened his
parachute and floated back to Earth.

According to Guinness World Records, Eustace
officially set the record for highest free fall
parachute jump. Always the scientist, he hoped
his feat would inspire further study of Earth's
atmosphere. "I hope we've encouraged others to
explore this part of the world about which we still
know so little," he said.

FACT

At sea level, the speed
of sound is 1,225 kilometres
(761.2 miles) per hour. That
rate changes depending on
temperature, altitude and
other conditions.

altitude distance above
sea level

atmosphere mixture of gases
that surrounds Earth

velocity rate of speed

CHAPTER 4

THROUGH WATER, OVER LAND

Not all record-setting stunts are about speed, power and showmanship. Sometimes they are slow, lonely tests of endurance. These stunts often pit people against the power of nature.

Chloë McCardel took on the Atlantic Ocean near the Bahamas. The 29-year-old Australian could swim incredibly long distances. In October 2014 she set out to swim 128 kilometres (79.5 miles).

Hour after hour, in daylight and dark, McCardel swam. She did not use flippers, a snorkel or a wet suit. She was followed by helpers in a support boat. They could give her snacks and drinks. They also watched for sharks. But McCardel could not get out of the water or hold onto the boat to rest. For more than 42 hours she kept going. Exhaustion and **dehydration** wore her down. She suffered painful jellyfish stings. The salt water made her tongue and face swell.

dehydration extreme loss of water from the body

McCardel suffered 15 jellyfish stings during her record-setting swim.

Finally, McCardel had to call it quits. She was just 2 kilometres (1.2 miles) from her goal. But her swim of 126 kilometres (78.3 miles) still set a world record. Her husband, Paul McQueeney, called it the "gutsiest effort I've ever seen in my life."

Steve Fisher powered through tough rapids to take first place in the 2002 Gorge Games Men's Extreme Kayak event in Oregon, USA.

WITH A PADDLE

Africa's Congo River has the world's biggest rapids, the Inga Rapids. They are 80 kilometres (50 miles) long, powerful and deadly. As of 2010, no boat had ever successfully navigated them, though some adventurers had died trying. In 2011 South African daredevil Steve Fisher and three other expert kayakers made their own attempt.

The Inga Rapids proved as big a test as the team had hoped – and feared. The water rushed along as fast as 48 kilometres (30 miles) per hour. Huge waves piled up on boat-breaking rocks. It had unpredictable surges, whirlpools and waterfalls.

The team had to plan its way through each stretch of rapids. A helicopter team scouted ahead and radioed back the safest route. But one mistake could send a paddler into water that might never spit them out.

It took four days for the group to run the Inga Rapids. Everyone made it safely, but there were some close calls. "It felt like the river was literally trying to kill us at every single twist and turn," said team member Tyler Bradt.

THE YOUNGEST RECORD BREAKERS

Adults are not the only people breaking records. Each year kids try to be the youngest to test their courage against big challenges. Here are just a few examples.

Mount Everest is the tallest mountain in the world. In 2014 Malavath Poorna of India became the youngest girl to climb it. She was 13 years, 11 months old. American Jordan Romero was the youngest boy to climb it in 2010. He was 13 years, 10 months old.

American Sierra "Monkey" Burror hiked the 4,184-kilometre (2,600-mile) Pacific Crest Trail with her mum in 2012. She was the youngest ever to walk the entire route from Mexico to Canada. Burror celebrated her ninth birthday during the trek.

From 2010 to 2012, Laura Dekker of the Netherlands sailed solo around the world. She was just 16 when she finished.

In 2014 American Matt Guthmiller became the youngest pilot to fly solo around the globe. He was 19.

FACT

Guinness World Records no longer reports some records for dangerous feats by young people. It fears such records encourage dangerous stunts.

CHAPTER 5

AMAZING FILM STUNTS

James Bond films have a history of wild stunts. But one stuntman went above and beyond in the 1995 thriller *GoldenEye*. Wayne Michaels was the stuntman standing in for Pierce Brosnan. He took a bungee jump off Switzerland's Verzasca Dam. The dam stands 220 metres (720 feet) tall – taller than many skyscrapers. In the film, Bond seemed to fall forever before the elastic cable strapped to his ankles absorbed the force of the drop. He reached the ground and made his escape.

The jump set the world height record for bungee jumping off a fixed structure. It also helped jump-start a bungee-jumping craze around the world.

Films are not usually in the business of breaking world records, unless they are for most ticket sales. Still, daredevils play important roles by filling films with action.

FACT

The highest film free fall from a building was made for the 1981 movie *Sharky's Machine*. Stuntman Dar Robinson dropped 67 metres (220 feet) into a giant air bag.

The bungee jump in the movie *GoldenEye* had a 7.5-second free fall.

NO STUNT DOUBLE REQUIRED

Most film stunts are performed by stunt artists. These performers have the training and experience to stage fights, falls and crashes safely and with style. Early film actors performed many of their own stunts. Their brushes with disaster got big gasps and laughs from the audience.

Chinese actor Jackie Chan has continued the tradition of performing his own stunts. Chan became a film star by mixing martial arts moves with comic twists. His furious and funny fight scenes left him with many injuries and broken bones.

Chan has made more than 100 films during his action-filled career. He got bruised tumbling down the sloped side of a 21-storey skyscraper. He burned his hands sliding down a pole covered in Christmas lights. He broke his skull falling out of a tree. In 2012 Guinness World Records announced that Chan had earned his own world record: "Most Stunts by a Living Actor".

Jackie Chan performs a stunt for his 2003 film *The Medallion*.

THE FUTURE OF STUNTS

More and more, computer-generated imagery (CGI) has replaced real stunts in films. Computer animation can fill a scene with complete destruction without anyone risking a scratch.

But there will always be a place for real stunts done by real people. People feel a special buzz when a daredevil is putting everything on the line. They may even see someone accomplish what has never been done before.

GLOSSARY

altitude distance above sea level

atmosphere mixture of gases that surrounds Earth

concussion injury to the brain caused by a hard blow to the head

dehydration extreme loss of water from the body

endurance ability to continue when tired or in pain

generation group of people born and living at about the same time

obstacle something that gets in the way or prevents someone from doing something

showmanship ability to entertain and perform

spectacle big public show

sponsor person or company that supports a project

velocity rate of speed

FIND OUT MORE

BOOKS

A Daredevil's Guide to Stunts (Daredevils' Guides), Steve Goldworthy (Capstone, 2013)

Being a Stuntman (Top Jobs), Isabel Thomas (Wayland, 2012)

Mind-Blowing Movie Stunts (Wild Stunts), Joe Tougas (Raintree, 2015)

WEBSITES

British Action Academy: Stunt Training
www.britishactionacademy.com/screen-action-courses/stunt-training/

How to Become a Stunt Performer
www.plotr.co.uk/careers/stunt-performer/overview/

Stunt Performers and Coordinators
www.jigs.org.uk/stunts/

COMPREHENSION QUESTIONS

1. What are some reasons that might drive someone to become a stunt person?

2. Why do you think people are so fascinated with dangerous stunts?

INDEX